LITURGICAL

M000076240

CHRISTMAS

Season of Wonder and Hope

Catherine Upchurch

Little Rock
Scripture Study

A ministry of the Diocese of Little Rock
in partnership with Liturgical Press

Nihil obstat: Msgr. Francis I. Malone, *Censor Librorum.*
Imprimatur: ✠ Anthony B. Taylor, Bishop of Little Rock, February 2, 2018.

Cover design by Ann Blattner. Cover photo: Getty Images. Used with permission.

Photos/illustrations: Pages 7, 10, 13, 14, 16, 18, 20, 22, 23, 25, 26, 29, 33, 36, 38, 39, 41, Getty Images. Used with permission. Page 12, Clifford M. Yeary.

Scripture texts, prefaces, introductions, footnotes, and cross references used in this work are taken from the *New American Bible, revised edition* © 2010, 1991, 1986, 1970 Confraternity of Christian Doctrine, Washington, DC and are used by permission of the copyright owner. All Rights Reserved. No part of the *New American Bible* may be reproduced in any form without permission in writing from the copyright owner.

Excerpt from the English translation of *The Roman Missal* © 2010, International Commission on English in the Liturgy Corporation. All rights reserved.

© 2018 by Little Rock Scripture Study, Little Rock, Arkansas. All rights reserved. No part of this book may be reproduced in any form or by any means without the written permission of the copyright holder. Published by Liturgical Press, Collegeville, Minnesota 56321. Printed in the United States of America.

ISBN: 978-0-8146-4401-0 (print); 978-0-8146-4425-6 (ebook)

Contents

Introduction

Alive in the Word brings you resources to deepen your understanding of Scripture, offer meaning for your life today, and help you to pray and act in response to God's word.

Use any volume of **Alive in the Word** in the way best suited to you.

- **For individual learning and reflection,** consider this an invitation to prayerfully journal in response to the questions you find along the way. And be prepared to move from head to heart and then to action.

- **For group learning and reflection,** arrange for three sessions where you will use the material provided as the basis for faith sharing and prayer. You may ask group members to read each chapter in advance and come prepared with questions answered. In this kind of session, plan to be together for about an hour. Or, if your group prefers, read and respond to the questions together without advance preparation. With this approach, it's helpful to plan on spending more time for each group session in order to adequately work through each of the chapters.

- For a parish-wide event or use within a larger group, provide each person with a copy of this volume, and allow time during the event for quiet reading, group discussion and prayer, and then a final commitment by each person to some simple action in response to what he or she learned.

This volume on the topic of Christmas is one of several volumes that explore **Liturgical Seasons**. Our church accents seasons within each year to help us enter into the story of salvation. This is commonly referred to as the liturgical calendar. Its purpose is not to mark the passage of time but to understand the overall mystery of salvation in Jesus Christ, from his incarnation and birth through his ministry, death, resurrection, and sending of the Spirit. By meditating on the themes of these various seasons in the church year, we are more fully able to live the mystery of Christ in our own lives.

Prologue

There's nothing quite like the satisfaction of the day *after* Christmas when the presents have been opened and "oohed and aahed" over, the chaos has settled, the meal eaten, clean dishes are ready to be put away, and the giant after-Christmas sales have already begun. Job well done, we may be thinking. Maybe, however, we need to revisit this from the perspective of the meaning of Christmas.

In our church's tradition, Christmas is not confined to the weeks leading up to December 25, ending on the day itself when the stores are finally closed for a rest. Christmas is not even the twenty-four-hour period from Christmas Eve through Christmas Day. In our tradition, Christmas is a season that begins on Christmas Eve and, for Roman Catholics, extends through the feast of the Baptism of the Lord.

The Christmas season includes the feasts of St. Stephen and St. John and the Holy Innocents and the Holy Family, as well as the Solemnities of the Blessed Virgin Mary, Mother of God, and the Epiphany. All of these serve as markers along the way, helping us to further reflect on the power of the nativity of the Lord, not simply as *a* special day but as a divine gift that changes *every* day throughout the year.

To heighten our appreciation of Christmas as a season, we focus on three New Testament passages in this book, passages that reveal the wonder and hope contained in a child's simple birth in Bethlehem centuries ago, and his birth in our hearts each day.

Marveling with the Shepherds

Begin by asking God to assist you in your prayer and study. Then read Luke 2:1-18, an account of the birth of Jesus.

Luke 2:1-18

[1]In those days a decree went out from Caesar Augustus that the whole world should be enrolled. [2]This was the first enrollment, when Quirinius was governor of Syria. [3]So all went to be enrolled, each to his own town. [4]And Joseph too went up from Galilee from the town of Nazareth to Judea, to the city of David that is called Bethlehem, because he was of the house and family of David, [5]to be enrolled with Mary, his betrothed, who was with child. [6]While they were there, the time came for her to have her child, [7]and she gave birth to her firstborn son. She wrapped him in swaddling clothes and laid him in a manger, because there was no room for them in the inn.

[8]Now there were shepherds in that region living in the fields and keeping the night watch over their flock. [9]The angel of the Lord appeared to them and the glory of the Lord shone around them, and they were struck with great fear. [10]The angel said to them, "Do not be afraid; for behold, I proclaim to you good news of great joy that will be for all the people. [11]For today in the city of David a savior has been born for you who is Messiah and Lord. [12]And this will be a sign for you: you will find an infant wrapped in swaddling clothes and lying in a manger." [13]And suddenly there was a multitude of the heavenly host with the angel, praising God and saying:

[14]"Glory to God in the highest
  and on earth peace to those on whom his
    favor rests."

[15]When the angels went away from them to heaven, the shepherds said to one another, "Let us go, then, to Bethlehem to see this thing that has taken place, which the Lord has made known to us." [16]So they went in haste and found Mary and Joseph, and the infant lying in the manger. [17]When they saw this, they made known the message that had been told them about this child. [18]All who heard it were amazed by what had been told them by the shepherds.

After a few moments of quiet reflection on Luke 2:1-18 consider the background information found in "Setting the Scene." This information will help you put the passage in context.

Setting the Scene

Gospels do more than simply communicate factual information about Jesus, the main character. They are tools for evangelization, meaning that they are written as an invitation to encounter and then to enter into a relationship with Jesus. Gospel writers tell the story for an audience that they are a part of, but do it in such a way that calls for a response even generations later.

The inspired writings attributed to Luke, which include the Gospel as well as the Acts of the Apostles, show a keen awareness of the world into which Jesus was born and the church was established. References to historical persons, events, and geographical locations demonstrate that Jesus entered into a specific set of circumstances as Good News for the real world. This lesson alone, that God comes to meet us in the reality of our lives, is one of the central truths of our lives as followers of Christ and is the heart of the Christmas message.

In the opening lines of his gospel, Luke indicates that he is writing down "in an orderly sequence" a narrative of the events surrounding Jesus. His writing style is methodical, allowing the story to unfold in a way that takes the reader on a journey—a journey from the promises made to Jewish ancestors to their fulfillment in the cross and resurrection of Jesus, and then in the Acts, on to the far corners of the world.

All eighty verses of the first chapter of Luke prepare the way for the birth of Jesus. There are two annunciations: one to Zechariah, the *"more metrical"*

husband of barren Elizabeth, and one to Mary, young and betrothed to Joseph. There are two canticles: one proclaimed by Mary while still pregnant and visiting Elizabeth and one proclaimed by Zechariah after the birth of his son John (the Baptist). In the midst of these pairings, John's birth to Elizabeth and Zechariah breaks ground for Jesus, the one for whom he will later prepare a way in the desert (Luke 3:1-20).

In chapter 1, Luke has taken the time to connect the new work of God coming in the birth of Jesus to the expectations building in God's people for centuries. Zechariah and Elizabeth evoke God's faithfulness to Israel for generations, while Mary and Joseph help us to transition into the time of the long-awaited Messiah. The stage is set for the birth of Jesus, the Messiah and Lord.

The passage from Luke 2:1-18 will be considered a few verses at a time in the section below. Occasional questions in this section and following sections may be used for personal reflection, journaling, or group discussion.

Understanding the Scene Itself

¹**In those days a decree went out from Caesar Augustus that the whole world should be en-**

rolled. [2]This was the first enrollment, when Quirinius was governor of Syria. [3]So all went to be enrolled, each to his own town. [4]And Joseph too went up from Galilee from the town of Nazareth to Judea, to the city of David that is called Bethlehem, because he was of the house and family of David, [5]to be enrolled with Mary, his betrothed, who was with child.

Jewish hopes for the Messiah, the anointed of God, included the expectation that he would come from the house of David, and David's family was from Bethlehem in the region of Judea. The prophet Micah, who ministered to God's people over seven hundred years before Jesus was born, had referred to Bethlehem as "least among the clans of Judah" and the place that would produce the "one who is to be ruler in Israel" (Mic 5:1).

At the time of the birth of Jesus, Israel was a small nation-state in the midst of many others that made up the Roman Empire. Caesar Augustus, also referred to as Octavian, was the Roman Emperor at this time (ca. 27 BC–AD 14). So great were his accomplishments—among them restoring peace after the assassination of Julius Caesar and establishing an imperial dynasty—that various historical records indicate he is referred to as "son of god" and even as "savior." We are meant to catch the irony that the child Jesus, born on the margins of society in an insignificant region of the empire, would be recognized as the true Savior and Son of God, and his rule would be like no other.

What messages about power are common today? Where have you discovered the Christian message in tension with the cultural messages about power?

Whether there was an actual census at the time is disputed by historians who cannot find any evidence, but we miss the point if that's all that consumes us. The evangelists crafted the story of Jesus to emphasize his significance. The journey of this couple from their home in Nazareth to the place of their family origin at a time when the region saw its own turmoil may prompt us to consider many journeys of significance, the greatest being God's journey from divinity to humanity, from heaven to earth, in the birth of his Son.

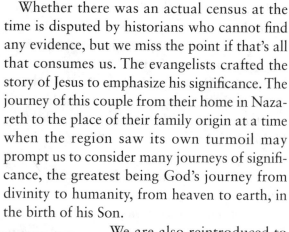

When has a physical journey helped you to discover or identify God's work in your life?

A retreat.

We are also reintroduced to the main characters—Joseph, his wife Mary, and the child still in her womb.

⁶**While they were there, the time came for her to have her child, ⁷and she gave birth to her first-born son. She wrapped him in swaddling clothes and laid him in a manger, because there was no room for them in the inn.**

It's a simple story line: circumstances shift as the newly betrothed couple makes their journey, simple and far from ideal arrangements are made for a birth, and the child's mother treats her son with the tenderness required of the moment.

Naturally, we imagine the scene, meaning we immediately conjure up images and the feelings that go along with them. People have been doing so since the story was first told. Through art and literature and music and pageants, we want to picture the scene, to capture some of the mix of anxiety and wonder that surely charged the air where Mary and Joseph found themselves. We want to see that child lying peacefully in a makeshift cradle. We want to hear the whisperings of his parents who are far from home. We may even want

to picture the innkeeper who would have heard the birth and maybe felt a twinge of regret that they were not given better conditions.

This manger in Bethlehem has been called the most famous feeding trough in history! A manger is basically a place for livestock to feed, most often thought of as a trough. Some of these feeding areas were actually located in an open lower level of a simple home built into a hillside, making it easy for sheep and goats and cows to enter when needed. This child, destined to be the savior as the angels will later proclaim (2:11), makes a bold statement about the human condition simply by being born in such simple surroundings.

The reference to Mary's "firstborn son" is quite intentional and has little to do with whether he may have had natural brothers and sisters. First of all, in ancient Judaism the firstborn son had certain rights according to Mosaic Law, rights to blessing and inheritance, and the firstborn was often dedicated to God much as firstfruits were offered to God at harvest. Secondly,

Jesus was laid in the place where cattle are fed, in a town whose name, Bethlehem, means "house of bread." In what ways does Jesus feed you?

Eucharist
Parables
Locutions
Mystically

by God's grace believers become sons and daughters of God, brothers and sisters to Jesus (see John 1:12-13; Rom 8:16-17; Eph 1:5-6).

[8]Now there were shepherds in that region living in the fields and keeping the night watch over their flock. [9]The angel of the Lord appeared to them and the glory of the Lord shone around them, and they were struck with great fear. [10]The angel said to them, "Do not be afraid; for behold, I proclaim to you good news of great joy that will be for all the people. [11]For today in the city of David a savior has been born for you who is Messiah and Lord."

Shepherd's Field near Bethlehem is a popular pilgrimage site today. Whether or not it is the actual field, there is no doubt of the devotion many feel in regard to these lowly dedicated keepers of flocks. Shepherds were considered among the lowest of laborers but, for yet another connection with tradition, we know Israel's most revered king, David, shepherded flocks in that region as well (1 Sam 16:4-13).

In Luke's account, the shepherds are the first to hear a proclamation of the birth of the savior, the Messiah, the Lord. An "angel of the Lord" and "the glory of the Lord" produced fear in them. The Greek word *phobos* is translated here as fear which we might understand as being scared, but may also be translated as reverence or wonderment. It's easy to imagine that the shepherds, busy about their nightly routines, might experience a mixture of both in response to such an extraordinary event.

"Be not afraid" is among the most frequently used responses throughout the Bible. Far from being a stock answer, these three words signal that God is doing something new, something out of the ordinary. These three words also remind those being addressed—those in the story and readers now—that God is in control. If the fear is associated with the feeling of being frozen in terror, God proclaims that such fear is needless. If the fear is in fact wonder and awe, God invites the kind of trust that will not leave us unchanged.

In the Roman Empire, it was customary upon the birth of an emperor's son to proclaim the good news that peace and prosperity would follow in his footsteps. Politicians and poets spread this good news across the land. In the scene from Luke's gospel the proclamation of Good News comes from an angel and is given to the lowliest of people to spread throughout the land.

The child will be savior, Messiah, and Lord. Savior was a term often given to rulers in the Greco-Roman world. In this context, however, the "savior" is a liberator, much in the line of Moses who was God's instrument of freedom for those enslaved in Egypt. In the gospel accounts we will see Jesus act as liberator to those who are oppressed, caught in their own sinfulness,

In the *Magnificat* (Luke 1:46-55), Mary proclaims that God "has thrown down the rulers from their thrones but lifted up the lowly" (v. 52). How is this illustrated in the scene at Shepherd's Field? *Not to "rulers"*

When has fear created an obstacle to your spiritual growth? When has God's assurance transformed your fear?

Savior
Messiah
Lord

Samari
tan woman

and ostracized. As Messiah, the child will grow to proclaim and establish God's kingdom as had been promised to David centuries before. As Lord, Jesus possesses true power and authority, given by the Father, a power that surpasses that of emperors and kings, a power that is divine. These titles serve as an introduction to his entire ministry and the meaning of his life, death, and resurrection.

[12]"And this will be a sign for you: you will find an infant wrapped in swaddling clothes and lying in a manger." [13]And suddenly there was a multitude of the heavenly host with the angel, praising God and saying:

[14]"Glory to God in the highest
and on earth peace to those on whom his favor rests."

Having just been told that the child is Savior, Messiah, and Lord, the shepherds are told to look for a sign. Surely they would have expected some sign of royalty or power, perhaps a throne or a temple or a castle. Instead, the sign is that simple manger where the baby is lying. This contrast or paradox is only the first of many that will be part of the life of Jesus, and the lives of his followers. He was a humble man but filled with authority, he was the bringer of truth who also offered mercy and forgiveness, and he was the healer and sinless one who nonetheless faced a horrible death.

Caesar Augustus, the emperor noted at the start of this account, was known for establishing a period of peace, Pax Romana, which allowed the empire to breathe a short sigh of relief. It was a time when borders were protected and it was relatively tranquil. Now, in the field where shepherds kept their watch, the angels proclaim that God's glory is reflected in the peace embodied in Christ. This is not the mere absence of war, but the promise of wholeness and restoration, a peace that surpasses that of Caesar Augustus.

How could you use this Christmas season to be an ambassador of the kind of peace Jesus offers?

¹⁵**When the angels went away from them to heaven, the shepherds said to one another, "Let us go, then, to Bethlehem to see this thing that has taken place, which the Lord has made known to us." ¹⁶So they went in haste and found Mary and Joseph, and the infant lying in the manger. ¹⁷When they saw this, they made known the message that had been told them about this child. ¹⁸All who heard it were amazed by what had been told them by the shepherds.**

The wonderment of the shepherds did not leave them in a stupor, having experienced a manifestation of God's presence, having been told of a long-awaited Messiah. They moved, they set their feet in the direction of Bethlehem to see with their own eyes what had taken place.

It might be fair to say that an encounter with the divine never leaves us without a mission? For the shepherds, the mission was to make known the message, giving witness to what they had seen and heard. They represent not only all who spread the Good News but the very kind of people who need to hear the message that their Savior has arrived. Their mission, and ours, is to evangelize. We tell what God has done among us, what we have seen, how we have been changed in the encounter.

Apostolate

Those who heard the news from the shepherds were "amazed." Amazement can take the shape of being surprised but it can also mean that someone is incredulous, wondering if the event lacks credibility. Further, the root word is "maze," so to be amazed may mean there is lingering confusion. Those who were amazed may or may not have moved into faith and trust. The message of the shepherds invited them to wonder at God's goodness and to have hope that the promises of God were being fulfilled. Will those who are amazed take steps toward the manger? Will we?

What steps are you taking that will draw you closer to the manger and the gift that it holds?

Praying the Word / Sacred Reading

Spend some time reflecting on a nativity scene, perhaps one in your parish or one in your home.

- *Why does this scene capture your imagination?* color rural

- *How might you have reacted if you were one of the shepherds?* proud

- *Who would you have told first when you left the manger?* Flocks owner

As you close your reflection time, speak to God about the shepherds and ask how you might be like them. Ask for the grace to open yourself to the glory of God in the normal course of your daily routine. contemplation

Living the Word

The child lying in a manger was a sign for the shepherds, a confirmation that what they had been told was real, a sign that God brought heaven to earth.

Where are the mangers in your life, the places that serve to remind you of God's faithfulness and presence? If they are physical places, take time to visit one or two of them to recall God's care. If they are places in your heart, talk about them with your family or close friends. These are reminders of the marvelous gift of God's Son, and also reminders of our call to evangelize.

Saints Nature/sun baby

Journeying with the Magi

Invite God to assist you in your prayer and study. Then read Matthew 2:1-12, a second account of the birth of Jesus.

Matthew 2:1-12

¹When Jesus was born in Bethlehem of Judea, in the days of King Herod, behold, magi from the east arrived in Jerusalem, ²saying, "Where is the newborn king of the Jews? We saw his star at its rising and have come to do him homage." ³When King Herod heard this, he was greatly troubled, and all Jerusalem with him. ⁴Assembling all the chief priests and the scribes of the people, he inquired of them where the Messiah was to be born. ⁵They said to him, "In Bethlehem of Judea, for thus it has been written through the prophet:

⁶'And you, Bethlehem, land of Judah,
    are by no means least among the rulers of Judah;
since from you shall come a ruler,
    who is to shepherd my people Israel.'"

⁷Then Herod called the magi secretly and ascertained from them the time of the star's appearance. ⁸He sent them to

Bethlehem and said, "Go and search diligently for the child. When you have found him, bring me word, that I too may go and do him homage." [9]After their audience with the king they set out. And behold, the star that they had seen at its rising preceded them, until it came and stopped over the place where the child was. [10]They were overjoyed at seeing the star, [11]and on entering the house they saw the child with Mary his mother. They prostrated themselves and did him homage. Then they opened their treasures and offered him gifts of gold, frankincense, and myrrh. [12]And having been warned in a dream not to return to Herod, they departed for their country by another way.

> *The information provided below in "Setting the Scene" will help you move from reflection to understanding by providing background information.*

Setting the Scene

The Gospel of Matthew opens with seventeen verses that list the genealogy of Jesus, from Abraham through "Joseph, the husband of Mary." Right away, by providing such a lineage, the reader is alerted to the significance of the child to be born of this couple. He is the fulfillment of generations of Israel's hopefulness and God's faithfulness.

The actual birth of Jesus is not so much recounted as it is reported in Matthew's version of an annunciation (1:18-25). The emphasis in Matthew's account is on the dialogue between

the angel of the Lord and Joseph who, naturally, was initially caught off guard to find Mary pregnant. It is Joseph who receives the word that she is pregnant "through the holy Spirit," and who is told "do not be afraid." It is Joseph who is given the name Jesus for their child, literally meaning "God's help" or "God's salvation." It is Joseph who is told that the child is the fulfillment of Isaiah's prophecy and shall be called "Emmanuel," meaning "God is with us." It is Joseph who is obedient to God's plan and takes his betrothed into his home rather than divorcing her. It's as if we've flipped the script and are seeing the nativity played out from a different angle.

Only two of the gospels offer an infancy narrative and, while they both agree on Bethlehem as the site of the birth of Jesus, and that Jesus is the Messiah, the Savior, they differ in some important ways that will unfold as we look specifically at the beginning of chapter 2 in Matthew.

Matthew 2:1-12 will be considered a few verses at a time, with occasional questions in the margin for your reflection or group discussion.

Understanding the Scene Itself

¹**When Jesus was born in Bethlehem of Judea, in the days of King Herod, behold, magi from the east arrived in Jerusalem, ²saying, "Where is the**

newborn king of the Jews? We saw his star at its rising and have come to do him homage."

Matthew does not spend time identifying where Mary and Joseph lived prior to Jesus' birth in Bethlehem nor does he associate their being in Bethlehem with a census. This is not a matter of argument between Matthew and Luke but, rather, illustrates that each evangelist brings a particular purpose and insight to telling this all-important story.

King Herod, also known as Herod the Great, was king of Judea from 37 to 4 BC. (A later sixth century miscalculation in determining the Roman calendar explains how Jesus could have been born while Herod was still king.) Known for his monumental building campaigns in the region, including the rebuilt Jerusalem temple and a working aqueduct that carried water through the Judean desert, Herod was also known for his cruelty, even executing his own family members. A convert to Judaism and the local representative of the Romans who controlled the region, he was not trusted by the general population.

Situating the birth of Jesus during the waning years of King Herod's reign helps to draw the contrast between the peaceful birth of a newborn king and the brutality of an aging monarch.

While later tradition assigned the names Caspar, Balthasar, and Melchior to the magi, the

Sometimes we recognize a great truth only in contrast. When has the message of the Gospel been clearer to you in contrast to the messages of the world around us?

biblical account itself never supplied their names. Nor do we know exactly their country of origin. We presume they are Gentiles since they do not seem to know the location of the Messiah's birth and have to call upon Jewish leaders to provide scriptural verification.

The word magi (from the Greek word *magos* or *magoi*) can be used to speak about the Persian priestly class or Eastern magicians or even astrologers. Given that they are following a star, most assume they were indeed astrologers who read the signs and knew to come seeking him.

What is clear is that the magi have a purpose to their journey: they have come to give homage to this newborn king. Right away, we are being told that their intentions are not only honorable but most appropriate.

[3]When King Herod heard this, he was greatly troubled, and all Jerusalem with him. [4]Assembling all the chief priests and the scribes of the people, he inquired of them where the Messiah was to be born. [5]They said to him, "In Bethlehem of Judea, for thus it has been written through the prophet:

[6]'And you, Bethlehem, land of Judah,
     are by no means least among the rulers of Judah;
since from you shall come a ruler,
     who is to shepherd my people Israel.'"

[7]Then Herod called the magi secretly and ascertained from them the time of the star's appearance. [8]He sent them to Bethlehem and said, "Go and search diligently for the child. When you

**have found him, bring me word, that I too may
go and do him homage."**

In stark contrast to the magi who wish to
worship and honor the new king, Herod is
"greatly troubled," no doubt threatened, to hear
of a potential rival, even one who is only days
old. It seems that Herod has succumbed to the
worst aspects of jealousy, an emotion that is
often rooted in insecurity or fear or disinforma-
tion. It rears its head most often when a person
feels threatened in some way.

In Herod's case, the potential for loss of power
and status overwhelmed any good judgment he
might have exercised. Although he indicates that
he wishes also to give homage to the child, we
know that eventually he will seek to eliminate
his future competition and will even go so far
as to order the execution of all male infants and
toddlers in Bethlehem and the surrounding area
(Matt 2:16-17). All this because the birth of a
child was hailed as a fulfillment of Israel's hopes
and God's promise to shepherd his people.

What experiences of envy or jealousy have taught you valuable lessons about human nature and perspective?

The author indicates
that the people of Jeru-
salem were troubled as
well. How are we to make
sense of this? If they did
not trust Herod, even
feared him, wouldn't a
possible replacement be
good news to them? Or
are they troubled for

other reasons, perhaps the potential upheaval that could leave them insecure? Or is this a reference to the religious leaders in Jerusalem, the scribes and chief priests who, by the time of Jesus' public ministry, opposed him so often?

What is clear is that the birth of Jesus would change the world. It would change Herod's world, the world of Jewish leaders and the world of ordinary citizens. It would change the world of Mary and Joseph, of his followers in his adult years. It would even change the world generations later in cultures that are widely varied.

[9]After their audience with the king they set out. And behold, the star that they had seen at its rising preceded them, until it came and stopped over the place where the child was. [10]They were overjoyed at seeing the star, [11]and on entering the house they saw the child with Mary his mother. They prostrated themselves and did him homage. Then they opened their treasures and offered him gifts of gold, frankincense, and myrrh.

The sign that the magi follow is a star, the "star they had seen at its rising." Speculation swirls around the nature of this star. Is it a comet? A meteor? The convergence of two planets? Matthew is not interested in astronomy and does not intend to explain it so that a twenty-first-century audience can identify the phenomenon. His concern is, rather, that listeners and readers will understand that this child is important, even royal.

In the ancient Mediterranean world, it was believed that heavenly signs would often mark the emergence or birth of a great leader. From the Jewish viewpoint, Matthew may also have in mind the story of the prophet Balaam who centuries earlier was summoned by the king of Moab to curse the Israelites. Instead, he offers extensive blessings and predicts, "A star shall advance from Jacob, and a scepter shall rise from Israel" (Num 24:17).

In this story from Matthew, the magi recognize that the star itself is not important; it is only a sign that points to the birth of the child whom they will worship. In the biblical tradition, signs always serve as evidence of the divine, pointing beyond themselves to the author of the sign. For the magi, the star serves to guide them not just to a place but into an experience of wonder.

> SIGNS always serve as evidence of the divine.

The response of the magi demonstrates that joy is the purest sign of wonder and the clearest pathway to hope. That which causes us deep joy opens our hearts to God's work in our lives and in the larger world. Such joy reminds us that, even when evidence is to the contrary, we have

What does joy look like to you? What mental image or memory comes to mind?

these glimmers of hope, these moments of clarity that show us evidence of God's handiwork and intention.

The magi come prepared with the disposition of awe and wonder that takes them to the ground in homage. Their exotic gifts for this newborn child reflect their belief that they are in the presence of royalty.

When has your experience of God been enhanced by the attitude you bring with you?

¹²And having been warned in a dream not to return to Herod, they departed for their country by another way.

Matthew's birth narrative begins with the introduction of Herod and returns to him again as the scene closes. Were we to read on (Matt 2:13-23), we would see that the magi were right in avoiding a return visit to him. Seeking to destroy any future threats to his power, Herod orders the massacre of innocent children in the region, forcing the Holy Family into exile in nearby Egypt. They would not return until Herod and his henchmen no longer held power and Herod himself had died.

Dreams play a significant role in the story— the dream that gave Joseph the courage to take Mary into his home when he could have divorced her, the dream that warned the new father to escape with his small family for safety, the dream that informed them that it was safe to return to Israel. In both the Old and New Testaments, dreams serve to reveal God's will and direction. These dreams are vehicles used to assure us that the story of salvation history is directed by God and is not merely a collection of chance happenings occurring in the lives of the Bible's characters.

Modern readers would do well to remember that the stories of the birth of Jesus were written and gathered not as the events themselves unfolded but only after the death and resurrection of Jesus had occurred. Only then did the early evangelists begin to explore his beginnings. It makes sense that their experience of the final events of Jesus' life would be the lens through which they understood all the events that came before. Through the lens of his passion and death they saw his birth and so we find shadows of that impending horror even in the way the birth narratives are written. But we also find the brightness of the resurrection show up along the way.

How does God usually get your attention?

In the utter darkness of night, in a sky filled with twinkling bursts of light, Matthew tells us that one star stood out and led a group of wise foreigners to a place that was unknown to them. That star, and the response of the magi, reminds us that light has much more power than darkness, that hope must outweigh fear, that wonder leads the way to faith.

Praying the Word / Sacred Reading

You may wish to read the passage from Matthew 2:1-12 again, imagining the purposeful journey of the magi, or putting yourself in the place of Joseph and Mary who receive these unknown travelers, or even positioning yourself in Herod's service as you hear the magi inquire about the child that is born.

Allow such a reading to lead you into prayer and reflection.

You may also wish to pray using these words:

God of all creation,

You set the stars in the sky to illuminate the
    earth,
      announcing that darkness will never have
        the last word.
You stirred Abraham's imagination when you
    invited him
      to count the starts if he could, promising
        him sons and daughters.

You inspired the psalmists to look to the
    heavens
      and ponder your power and your mercy.
Your prophets described the effects of sin as
    a sky without stars
      and the promises of God as plentiful as the
        starry nights.

You placed a star in the sky
      to guide people to worship your son, Jesus.
It is this star that still shines brightly
      and still leads the way to you.

Teach us to look to the heavens and observe
    your glory,
      and then take to the road to find you
        already in our midst.

Stir within us the desire to be with you and
    the courage to seek you.
Humble us in awe of your presence here
    with us.
Shape our lives to reflect your light in a world
    in need of it.

Living the Word

Interestingly, in both Matthew and Luke, the earliest visitors were considered outsiders in some way—the shepherds were among the poor and disadvantaged while the magi were not part of the covenant community of Israel. Both sets of visitors step out of their routine and make a great effort. Both exhibit joy. Both demonstrate what faith will look like as they adore Jesus and offer him their gifts.

- *Who are the "outsiders" who might be exemplifying what it means to seek Jesus and to honor him? Pay attention in your neighborhood and your place of work and see whose lives are giving honor to God.*

- *While we are not all called to make a physical journey as the magi did, we are nonetheless called to journey in faith as we are continually being shaped as disciples. We have to be willing to let go of familiar ways of acting and change our routines to appreciate God's presence with us.*

- *How would you describe your journey of faith?*

- *Are you willing to go further than what is comfortable as the magi did?*

- *Are you prepared to gaze in wonder at God's gift?*

- *Are you traveling with hope for what will be?*

God Made Visible

Invite God to assist you in your prayer and study. Then read the opening verses of the First Letter of John.

1 John 1:1-5
¹What was from the beginning,
   what we have heard,
   what we have seen with our eyes,
   what we looked upon
   and touched with our hands
   concerns the Word of life—
²for the life was made visible;
   we have seen it and testify to it
   and proclaim to you the eternal life
   that was with the Father and was made visible to us—

³what we have seen and heard
we proclaim now to you,
so that you too may have fellowship with us;
for our fellowship is with the Father
and with his Son, Jesus Christ.
⁴We are writing this so that our joy may be complete.

⁵Now this is the message that we have heard from him and proclaim to you: God is light, and in him there is no darkness at all.

The information found in "Setting the Scene" will help to fill in the context for this letter from John.

Setting the Scene

The books known to us as the First, Second, and Third Letters of John share some common themes and language with the Gospel According to John. For the most part, scholars believe that the gospel account would have been written prior to these three letters and that the writer or writers shared a common heritage linked to John the Evangelist. The writing reflected a time toward the end of the first century as Christianity was being more firmly established apart from Judaism where it had been born.

Actually, what we refer to as 1 John or the First Letter of John does not actually contain some of the standard features of ancient letters. There is no formal greeting or opening address at the start and it ends rather abruptly. We can deduce, however, that this material was written to address a division within the community, referenced in 1 John 2:18-23. This section speaks of those who were once members of the community but have left or denied Christ. In fact the author speaks of "antichrists" and in this context they are those who deny that Jesus is the Christ, the anointed one of God.

This First Letter of John begins, as does the Gospel According to John, with a prologue about the Word of God made flesh. The prologue found in John's gospel emphasizes the Word's preexistence with God and his coming in time to dwell among us. The letter focuses more directly on the experience of God living in the flesh among God's people.

The prologue of 1 John is compact, found in four verses, and is followed by the very common Johannine theme associating God with light. While these verses are often found in the Lectionary during the Easter season, they also provide a particular appreciation for Christ that is welcome in the season of Christmas.

Take time to read John 1:1-18, the prologue to the Fourth Gospel. Make note of the similarities you find with the prologue to the First Letter of John.

By considering the passages a verse at a time, the connections to our Christmas reflection will become more obvious.

Understanding the Scene Itself

[1]**What was from the beginning,
   what we have heard,
   what we have seen with our eyes,
   what we looked upon
   and touched with our hands
   concerns the Word of life—**

Both Genesis and the Gospel of John begin with the phrase, "In the beginning." Genesis is laying out the beginning of the cosmos, describing the purposeful ordering of creation, through the breath of God that spoke and all things came into being. The Gospel of John calls forth that same sense of cosmic beginnings, assuring readers that God's creative Word, now taking on flesh, is creating all things new once again. This First Letter of John is calling forth both of these images when he says "what was from the beginning . . . concerns the Word of life."

In the early church, and in various periods of history since then, there are signs of an overemphasis on either the divinity or the humanity of Jesus the Christ.

The Nicene Creed, written in AD 325 and fine-tuned in a series of councils in the following century, consistently emphasized that Jesus is fully human and fully divine.

How does the Nicene Creed use language and metaphors to help us state our belief in the two natures of Jesus Christ?

I believe in one Lord Jesus Christ,
the Only Begotten Son of God,
born of the Father before all ages.
God from God, Light from Light,
true God from true God,
begotten, not made, consubstantial with
    the Father;

through him all things were made.
For us men and for our salvation
he came down from heaven,
and by the Holy Spirit was incarnate of the
    Virgin Mary,
and became man.

Holding that tension together has always been a rather difficult concept for our minds and so we sometimes emphasize one over the other. It is possible that by the late first century, the writer of First John is giving a bit of a corrective to those who were discounting the humanity of Christ.

In this first verse, the human senses serve as a witness to his humanity—what we have heard, what we have seen, what we have touched. John is saying the incarnation, the "flesh and bones" nature of Christ, is real, just as real as his eternity, his being with God from the beginning. John is also assuring his audience that he is speaking not just on his own behalf but as part of those who have faithfully guarded and handed on the core Christian teaching of the incarnation. The repeated use of "us," "our," and "we" stands in opposition to others who would deny Christ—especially in his fully human and fully divine natures.

This first verse directs all the attention toward the "Word of life." For what purpose does God send his Son into our midst, taking on the human condition? The purpose is life, "eternal life" as we will read in the next verse, or "abundant life" as in John 10:10.

What tends to prevent you from experiencing the fullness of life given by Christ?

God
Man

²for the life was made visible;
  we have seen it and testify to it
  and proclaim to you the eternal life
  that was with the Father and was made visible
    to us—

The life that was made visible is the Son, the child born in Bethlehem who grew to maturity in Israel and who made it his mission to proclaim that life was always victorious over death. The Christian mission is to do as the writer says he has done—to see and recognize and testify and proclaim this Word of life who is Jesus.

The First Letter of John does not recount the actual birth of Jesus but does witness to the birth of Jesus in the hearts of believers. John is proclaiming not just the truth he was told but the truth he has experienced. It is this truth, the truth of Jesus taking on flesh and dwelling with us still, that continues to offer the gift of life in the here and now and into eternity.

What experiences have helped you claim more deeply the faith you profess in Jesus?

Los

Depression

³what we have seen and heard
  we proclaim now to you,
    so that you too may have fellowship with us;
    for our fellowship is with the Father
    and with his Son, Jesus Christ.

4We are writing this so that our joy may be complete.

The "fellowship" (*koinōnia* in Greek) that John refers to in verse 3 can also be expressed as communion or partnership or even participation. The union we experience with God because of Jesus Christ is as intimate as between a parent and a child. Such love is what Jesus came to make visible; such love is the essence of our relationship with the Father and our relationship with one another. This verse is a reminder that at the core of Christianity is the experience of God loving the world so much that he gave his only Son (John 3:16).

In the Gospel of John (15:1-17) we also find this experience described when Jesus speaks of himself as the true vine and issues the call to remain on the vine, to abide or dwell with Jesus as he abides with us. Our experience of God is not something that remains at arms' length but rather an actual organic relationship that transforms the present moment. It is the source of joy; it is rooted in love; it empowers love in return.

The Bible is filled with the invitation to joy. The psalms speak repeatedly of joy in the presence of God, in remembering God's mercy and believing in God's promises (e.g., Pss 16:11; 30:5-6; 71:23; 119:111). The

prophets hold out the promise of joy as God's people repent of their sin or return from exile (e.g, Isa 49:13; 56:12). And the New Testament itself gives witness to the joy that is a hallmark of Jesus' followers, from the inclusion of joy in the list of the fruit of the Spirit in Galatians 5 to the prison cell of Paul who still calls for joy in his letter to the Philippians.

For the Christian, joy is both a gift from God and an act of the will to submit to God, to see the world as God sees it, and to rest assured that God's very presence in us and in and among all things shapes our hearts and minds and even has the power to shape our world.

To what extent does joy stand out as a characteristic of your parish or family? Think of some concrete examples.

⁵Now this is the message that we have heard from him and proclaim to you: God is light, and in him there is no darkness at all.

The writer's message is not his own; it comes from Jesus Christ and it concerns the very nature of God: "God is light, and in him there is no darkness at all."

Six centuries earlier, the prophet Isaiah had announced God's message to those in Babylon. Their long exile was coming to an end and God wanted to assure his people that they had a service to offer the world. Isaiah spoke of them being called for justice to serve as "a light to the nations" and he went on to outline the mission of freeing prisoners and opening the eyes of the blind (Isa 42:6-7). Several chapters later the prophet says it is too little for them to be looking only to their own rescue but that God says, "I will make you a light to the nations" (Isa 49:6).

Jesus is that light living in the midst of the world, offering God's truth and justice. It is not enough that we only look sentimentally at the manger or gaze upon the stars for direction. Like Jesus, we are to reflect that light of God for all to see. We take the wonder and awe we experience at the sheer gift of God in his Son, we invest in the mission that Jesus himself was given, and we know there is a reason for hope even in darkness.

It is quite natural to be drawn to light in the midst of varying degrees of darkness. Who hasn't reacted warmly to a shaft of light coming through the shady deeps of a forest? Or the emergence of bright clouds following a storm? Or the first flames of a fire at a nighttime campsite? These moments of warmth and clarity serve as metaphors for the role of Christ in the world, and by extension, for our role as well.

For followers of Jesus, every day is Christmas. Every day affords the opportunity to search for him, to find him in our midst, and to grow up to carry on his mission. Every day there is need for God's goodness and mercy and justice and peace. Every day God offers light to a world in darkness, and many times that light will come through us. This is the Christian mission.

Both the shepherds and the magi had to leave the manger to spread the news of Jesus. How are you being called to go beyond the simplicity of Jesus' birth to proclaim his radical message of love?

Praying the Word / Sacred Reading

Take some time to select one verse from 1 John 1:1-5. Read this verse aloud, slowly and prayerfully, several times.

- *What words linger in your mind and heart?*

- *What images come to you?*

- *What would you like to talk with God about as a result of this prayerful reading?*

You may also wish to pray with these words, adding your own . . .

Jesus, your birth leaves us breathless
    with its simplicity and power,
    all rolled into one in a simple manger.

Stir our hearts to adore, to pay homage, to be thankful,
    And then turn us toward the world that is so in need of the Good News.

In our minds and hearts may we allow you to grow up,
    to embrace all that it is to be human
    so that your grace touches every part of the human experience.

Most of all, as we experience the love you share with your Father,
    may our joy give light to the world,
    your light, your love, your goodness.

You are the reason for our hope,
    not just in this season but for all times.

Living the Word

In your life, who has been a trustworthy witness to the Word of life? Who has helped you to recognize the presence of Jesus in our midst? Find a way to thank them for this gift in your life—send a text, write a letter, visit with them in person, or remember them in conversation with others.

Do you think it might be possible to train yourself to look for the light even in the midst of darkness? How will you go about raising your awareness? Who might help you seek the light rather than fear the darkness?

What is it about the message and ministry of Jesus that gives you reason to hope? Make a list of the hopeful events or phrases or images from the gospel stories and take time to pray with these items on a regular basis.